SPECIAL AGENTS OF † CHRIST

A PRAYER BOOK FOR YOUNG ORTHODOX SAINTS

SPECIAL AGENTS OF CHRIST · 1 TIMOTHY 4:12

FROM THE AUTHOR OF *HEAR ME*

ANNALISA BOYD

SPECIAL AGENTS OF CHRIST:
A PRAYERBOOK FOR YOUNG ORTHODOX SAINTS

Original material copyright © 2012 by Annalisa Boyd
All Rights Reserved

Prayers are adapted from original ancient sources by the author.

All scripture quotations, unless otherwise indicated, are taken from the Holy Bible, New International Reader's Version®, NIrV® Copyright © 1995, 1996, 1998 by Biblica, Inc.™ Used by permission of Zondervan. All rights reserved worldwide. www.zondervan.com.

The "NIrV" and "New International Reader's Version" are trademarks registered in the United States Patent and Trademark Office by Biblica, Inc.™

Scripture quotations in Drill #2 are from the Orthodox Liturgy.

Published by   Conciliar Press
                   A division of Conciliar Media Ministries
                   P.O. Box 748
                   Chesterton, IN 46304

Printed in the United States of America

ISBN: 978-1-936270-55-2

Library of Congress Cataloging-in-Publication Data

Boyd, Annalisa.
Special agents of Christ : a prayer book for young Orthodox saints / Annalisa Boyd ; illustrated by Sheena Hisiro.
     p. cm.
ISBN 978-1-936270-55-2 (alk. paper)
1. Orthodox Eastern Church--Prayers and devotions--Juvenile literature.
2. Prayer books--Juvenile literature. 3. Christian children--Prayers and devotions--Juvenile literature. 4. Orthodox Eastern Church--Doctrines--Juvenile literature. 5. Bible--Biography. I. Title.

BX376.F5B69 2012
242'.82--dc23

                        2012018944

CONTENTS

PART TWO

SPECIAL
AGENTS
OF
CHRIST

INTRODUCTION

You are invited to be part of an amazing training camp found in the pages of this book. Special agents of Christ have been chosen to train you in the arts of spiritual battle against the enemy of the world. These agents have faced lions, been sold into slavery, and fought to the death for the sake of Christ. If you choose to accept this mission, you too will be trained as agents of Christ. You don't need to be "older," and on-the-job training is provided. This call is for YOU!

"Don't let anyone look down on you because you are young. Set an example for the believers in what you say and in how you live. Also set an example in how you love and in what you believe. Show the believers how to be pure." (1 Timothy 4:12)

ARE YOU READY?

9

PART ONE

OPERATIONS

PRAYERS FOR
ALL OCCASIONS

OPERATION 1

DAILY PRAYER

AGENT:

PROPHET DANIEL

CODE NAME:
Belteshazzar (bel-ta-shaz-ar)

FEAST DAY:
December 17

LIVED:
Old Testament

MISSION:
Pray every day no matter what.
Help the king.
Survive lions' den!

Agent Daniel was stolen from his people when he was young. His training in prayer helped him not only survive his capture, but become one of the wise men of his new country. The other wise men, however, hated Daniel because the king liked Daniel more than them. These sneaky men secretly asked the king to pass a new law forcing everyone to worship only the king or be thrown into a pit of hungry lions. What was Daniel to do? If he wouldn't worship the king, he would be killed! Faced with death, Daniel chose to pray.

Prayer is very important in the lives of young agents. For Daniel it was what God used to show His power to the king, the wicked wise men, and all the people of Babylon. You see, Daniel was thrown into that pit of hungry lions, but God closed their mouths and kept them from hurting His special agent. The king was so glad Daniel had been kept safe that he ordered everyone in his kingdom to pray to Daniel's God. As for the wicked wise men—well, those lions were still hungry, but not for long.

»*To find out more about Daniel's adventures, read the Book of Daniel in your Bible.*

MORNING PRAYERS

The Trisagion Prayers
(try-sah-gee-on means "three times holy" or "thrice holy")

In the Name of the Father, and of the Son, and of the Holy Spirit. Amen.

Glory to You, our God, glory to You.

O Heavenly King, O Comforter, the Spirit of Truth, who are in all places and fill all things; Treasury of good things and Giver of Life: Come and dwell in us, cleanse us from every stain, and save our souls, O gracious Lord.

Holy God, Holy Mighty, Holy Immortal, have mercy on us. Holy God, Holy Mighty, Holy Immortal, have mercy on us. Holy God, Holy Mighty, Holy Immortal, have mercy on us.

Glory to the Father, and to the Son, and to the Holy Spirit, now and ever and unto ages of ages. Amen.

All-holy Trinity, have mercy on us. Lord, cleanse us from our sins. Master, pardon our iniquities. Holy God, visit and heal our infirmities for Your Name's sake.

Lord, have mercy, Lord, have mercy, Lord, have mercy.

Glory to the Father, and to the Son, and to the Holy Spirit, now and ever and unto ages of ages. Amen.

Our Father, who are in heaven, hallowed be Your Name. Your Kingdom come; Your will be done on earth as it is in heaven. Give us this day our daily bread; and forgive us our trespasses as we forgive those who trespass against us; and lead us not into temptation, but deliver us from evil.

For Yours is the Kingdom, and the power, and the glory of the Father, and of the Son, and of the Holy Spirit, now and ever and unto ages of ages. Amen.

The Breastplate Prayer
(by St. Patrick)

I get up today through God's strength to direct me:
God's might to carry me, God's wisdom to guide me,
God's eye to look before me, God's ear to hear me,
God's way to lie before me, God's shield to protect me,
God's angels to defend me:
Against traps of devils,
Against wanting to do anything that goes against God,
Against anyone who wants me to fail, near or far, alone or in a group.

Christ with me, Christ in front of me,
Christ behind me, Christ in me,
Christ under me, Christ above me,
Christ on my right, Christ on my left,
Christ all around me, Christ in length, Christ in height,
Christ in the heart of everyone who thinks of me,
Christ in the mouth of everyone who speaks of me,
Christ in every eye that sees me,
Christ in every ear that hears me.

Salvation is of the Lord, Salvation is of the Lord.
Salvation is of Christ.
May Your Salvation, O Lord, be with us forever.

The Creed
("Creed" means "I believe")

I believe in one God, the Father Almighty, Maker of heaven and earth, and of all things visible and invisible.

And in one Lord Jesus Christ, the Son of God, the Only-begotten, begotten of the Father before all worlds; Light of Light, very God of very God, begotten, not made; of one essence with the Father, by whom all things were made:

Who for us men and for our salvation came down from heaven, and was incarnate of the Holy Spirit and the Virgin Mary, and became man;

And was crucified also for us under Pontius Pilate, and suffered and was buried;

And the third day He rose again, according to the Scriptures; and ascended into heaven, and sits at the right hand of the Father;

And He shall come again with glory to judge the living and the dead, whose Kingdom shall have no end.

And I believe in the Holy Spirit, the Lord and Giver of Life, who proceeds from the Father, who with the Father and the Son together is worshipped and glorified, who spoke by the Prophets;

And I believe in One Holy Catholic and Apostolic Church. I acknowledge one Baptism for the remission of sins and the life of the world to come.
Amen.

(This is where you say your own prayers and thank God for His blessings.)

Through the prayers of our holy Fathers, Lord Jesus Christ our God, have mercy on me and save me.

MIDDAY PRAYERS

The Trisagion Prayers

In the Name of the Father, and of the Son, and of the Holy Spirit. Amen.

Glory to You, our God, glory to You.

O Heavenly King, O Comforter, the Spirit of Truth, who are in all places and fill all things; Treasury of good things and Giver of Life: Come and dwell in us, cleanse us from every stain, and save our souls, O gracious Lord.

Holy God, Holy Mighty, Holy Immortal, have mercy on us. Holy God, Holy Mighty, Holy Immortal, have mercy on us. Holy God, Holy Mighty, Holy Immortal, have mercy on us.

Glory to the Father, and to the Son, and to the Holy Spirit, now and ever and unto ages of ages. Amen.

All-holy Trinity, have mercy on us. Lord, cleanse us from our sins. Master, pardon our iniquities. Holy God, visit and heal our infirmities for Your Name's sake.

Lord, have mercy, Lord, have mercy, Lord, have mercy.

Glory to the Father, and to the Son, and to the Holy Spirit, now and ever and unto ages of ages. Amen.

Our Father, who are in heaven, hallowed be Your Name. Your Kingdom come; Your will be done on earth as it is in heaven. Give us this day our daily bread; and forgive us our trespasses as we forgive those who trespass against us; and lead us not into temptation, but deliver us from evil.

For Yours is the Kingdom, and the power, and the glory of the Father, and of the Son, and of the Holy Spirit, now and ever and unto ages of ages. Amen.

Troparion for the Sixth Hour
("Troparion" means a short hymn)

O Christ my God, who at this hour stretched out Your loving arms upon the cross so that all men might be gathered unto You, help me and save me as I cry out to You. Glory to You, O Lord.

EVENING PRAYERS

The Trisagion Prayers

In the Name of the Father, and of the Son, and of the Holy Spirit. Amen.

Glory to You, our God, glory to You.

O Heavenly King, O Comforter, the Spirit of Truth, who are in all places and fill all things; Treasury of good things and Giver of Life: Come and dwell in us, cleanse us from every stain, and save our souls, O gracious Lord.

Holy God, Holy Mighty, Holy Immortal, have mercy on us.
Holy God, Holy Mighty, Holy Immortal, have mercy on us.
Holy God, Holy Mighty, Holy Immortal, have mercy on us.

Glory to the Father, and to the Son, and to the Holy Spirit, now and ever and unto ages of ages. Amen.

All-holy Trinity, have mercy on us. Lord, cleanse us from our sins. Master, pardon our iniquities. Holy God, visit and heal our infirmities for Your Name's sake.

Lord, have mercy, Lord, have mercy, Lord, have mercy.

Glory to the Father, and to the Son, and to the Holy Spirit, now and ever and unto ages of ages. Amen.

Our Father, who are in heaven, hallowed be Your Name. Your Kingdom come; Your will be done on earth as it is in heaven. Give us this day our daily bread; and forgive us our trespasses as we forgive those who trespass against us; and lead us not into temptation, but deliver us from evil.

For Yours is the Kingdom, and the power, and the glory of the Father, and of the Son, and of the Holy Spirit, now and ever and unto ages of ages. Amen.

The Creed

I believe in one God, the Father Almighty, Maker of heaven and earth, and of all things visible and invisible.

And in one Lord Jesus Christ, the Son of God, the Only-begotten, begotten of the Father before all worlds; Light of Light, very God of very God, begotten, not made; of one essence with the Father, by whom all things were made:

Who for us men and for our salvation came down from heaven, and was incarnate of the Holy Spirit and the Virgin Mary, and became man;

And was crucified also for us under Pontius Pilate, and suffered and was buried;

And the third day He rose again, according to the Scriptures; and ascended into heaven, and sits at the right hand of the Father;

And He shall come again with glory to judge the living and the dead, whose Kingdom shall have no end.

And I believe in the Holy Spirit, the Lord and Giver of Life, who proceeds from the Father, who with the Father and the Son together is worshipped and glorified, who spoke by the Prophets;

And I believe in One Holy Catholic and Apostolic Church.
I acknowledge one Baptism for the remission of sins and
the life of the world to come.
Amen.

PRAYER BEFORE SLEEP

Into Your hands, O Lord, I give my soul and my body.
Bless me with Yourself, have mercy on me, and bless me
with eternal life. Amen.

MY PRAYER LIST
OF FAMILY & FRIENDS

_____
_____
_____
_____
_____
_____
_____
_____
_____
_____
_____
_____
_____
_____
_____
_____
_____
_____
_____
_____
_____
_____

PRAYERS IN TIMES OF TROUBLE

AGENT:

JOSEPH THE ALL-COMELY

CODE NAME:
Zaphenath-Paneah
(zaf-uh-nath-puh-NEE-uh)

FEAST DAY:
March 31

LIVED:
Old Testament

MISSION:
Prayer warrior in times of trouble. Sold by brothers. Sent to jail. Interpreter of dreams. Pharaoh's right hand man.

Have you ever had "one of those days"? You know the kind—you forgot your lunch, the dog really did eat your homework, you can't find where you put your allowance, you got blamed for something you didn't do, and everyone seems mad at you? Those are called trials. If you've had trials, you're in good company with many of God's agents.

Agent Joseph was the youngest of ten brothers. Sound like fun? No way! He was his father's favorite, and his brothers didn't like that at all. His brothers were so jealous of him they sold him to slave traders. Now that's a bad day! After that, Joseph had many ups and downs. He became a servant, but his master put him in charge of all the land he owned. He was lied about and thrown into jail, but the jailer trusted him to take care of the whole jail. He was forgotten in jail, but was made Pharaoh's second-in-command when he told Pharaoh the meaning of his dream through God's power.

Trials can be very hard, and you may have gone through, or be going through, challenges much bigger than forgetting your lunch or losing your allowance. But God has a plan for you: even during those tough times, He has not forgotten you. Praying in times of trouble lets you call on the God of the universe for help. And as with St. Joseph the All-Comely, even though our enemies might mean our trials for evil, God can use anything for the good of those who love Him.

» *To find out what happened to Joseph and his brothers, read Genesis 37 and 39–40 in your Bible.*

PRAYERS WHEN YOU'RE AFRAID

O Lord Jesus Christ, rescue me from this great fear I am facing. The Holy Scriptures tell me, "For God has not given us a spirit of fear, but of power and of love and of a sound mind" (2 Timothy 1:7 NKJV). Thank You that You can take away my fear.

My Father in heaven, take all fear from my heart and mind and put Your love, joy, and peace there in its place.

Dear Lord, thank You that I can trust You when I am afraid. Amen.

PRAYERS FOR WHEN YOU'RE ANGRY

Dear Lord, help me to use kind words and actions even when I feel angry. Amen.

Lord Jesus Christ, help me to calm down and be peaceful on the inside so I can be kind on the outside. Amen.

Holy Spirit, help me to be slow to get angry and quick to forgive. Amen.

PRAYERS FOR TIMES OF TROUBLE

Holy Father, help me in the trial I am going through. Thank You that I can trust You even when I don't understand what is going on. Amen.

Dear Lord Jesus, the trial I am going through seems so heavy. I know You are strong enough to handle anything. Please give me the courage to trust You.

Holy Trinity, please help. Amen.

PRAYERS FOR WHEN YOU ARE LONELY

O Lord my God, thank You that You are always with me even if no one else seems to be. Amen.

Dear Lord, thank You that You hear my prayers. Amen.

My Father, help me to be a friend to others who might feel lonely. Amen.

PRAYERS FOR WHEN YOU ARE SICK

Lord Jesus, I feel sick. Please heal my body. Amen.

Dear Lord, thank You that I can trust You even when I'm sick. Please make me well. Amen.

Holy Trinity, please hear my prayer and heal me from my pain. Amen.

Holy God, heal Your servant so I can praise You in health. Amen.

A PRAYER WHEN YOU DON'T KNOW WHAT TO PRAY

(Based on a prayer of Philaret, Metropolitan of Moscow)

Dear Lord, I don't know what to pray. You know all my needs. I believe whatever You let happen is for my good and will bring me closer to You. I only want what You want for my life. Teach me how to pray. Amen.

PRAYERS FOR WHEN YOU'VE BEEN BLAMED FOR SOMETHING YOU DIDN'T DO

O Lord, my God and my hope, I am being blamed for something I have not done. Help me to trust You to take care of me even if I am not able to show I am not guilty. I choose to trust You no matter what. Amen.

When You were blamed for something You didn't do and were nailed to the cross, You did not get angry or even try to prove You were right. Help me now, O Lord, to follow Your example. Amen.

SITUATIONS TO PRAY FOR

_____

_____

_____

_____

_____

_____

_____

_____

_____

_____

_____

_____

_____

_____

_____

_____

_____

_____

_____

Lord, have mercy!

OPERATION 3

PRAYERS OF THANKS

AGENT:

ST. PAUL

CODE NAME:
Saul

FEAST DAY:
June 29

LIVED:
New Testament

MISSION:
Started as enemy of Christ.
Blinded, imprisoned, shipwrecked,
bitten by poisonous snake.
Encourager to agents of Christ
in all the churches.

A gent Paul started out as an enemy of Christ named Saul. He was there cheering on the crowd that killed St. Stephen (the first Christian killed for the sake of Christ). But God wanted to use him as His own agent.

First God had to get Saul's attention. He made him go blind. Saul had scales like a snake's on his eyes, and only the prayers of another agent of Christ could heal him through God's power. When Saul could see again, he wasted no time in becoming one of God's strongest agents. He changed his name to Paul and took up the mission of telling the world about Jesus. Paul faced many hard times, but was so thankful Jesus had saved him from the enemy that he preached without fear, even when he was put in jail!

Sometimes during a time of trouble, we forget to thank God for His many blessings. Saint Paul shows us we can be thankful no matter what the trial, because we have the God of the universe on our side.

» *To read more about Paul's shipwreck and snake bite, read Acts 27:1—28:10 in your Bible.*

THANKSGIVING FOR THOSE WHO CARE FOR ME

Thank you, O Lord, for the family You have put me in, whether parents, grandparents, guardians, birth family, or adopted family. Thank You for all who love and care for me and look after me. Bless them and keep them safe. Grant them the strength to walk in Your ways. Help me to show my thanks to them by my right actions and words. May I follow Your example, You who became a willing servant to mankind, and give my help and service to those who take care of me without complaining. Amen.

THANKSGIVING FOR BROTHERS & SISTERS

Thank You, my God and King, for my brothers and sisters. Show me how to love them the way You love them. I know I am not perfect. Sometimes I sin against You, but You love me anyway and show me great kindness. Help me to love them as You love me. Show me how to bless them with kind words and actions, even when they do things to make me mad. Thank You for placing them in my life. Amen.

Dear Lord, thank You that my brothers and sisters are also made in Your image. Amen.

Lord Jesus Christ, have mercy on (name of brother or sister).

THANKSGIVING FOR FRIENDS

Holy Father, thank You for my friends. Amen.

Lord God, bless my friend _____ today. Amen.

Father in Heaven, help me to be a good friend. Amen.

THANKSGIVING FOR HOW GOD PROVIDES FOR MY NEEDS

Thank You, O Lord, for the food I have for today. Amen.

Lord of heaven, thank You for clothes to wear and a safe place to sleep. Amen.

Dear Jesus, thank You for giving me what I need, and thank You for all the extras too. Please help me to share or give to others as You have given to me. Amen.

THANKSGIVING FOR RECOVERY FROM SICKNESS

Thank You, Lord, for making me well. Amen.

Dear Father, thank You for taking away my pain and giving me my strength back. Amen.

O Heavenly Doctor, help me to remember to pray now that I'm well. Amen.

THANKSGIVING FOR BEING RESCUED FROM TROUBLE

Holy Father, thank You for rescuing me from my trial. Amen.

Dear Lord Jesus, thank You for being strong enough to handle everything. Amen.

Holy Trinity, thank You for helping me in my time of need. Amen.

I THANK GOD FOR . . .

_____

_____

_____

_____

_____

_____

_____

_____

_____

_____

_____

_____

_____

_____

_____

_____

_____

_____

_____

_____

OPERATION 4

PRAYERS FOR FAMILY, FRIENDS, AND ENEMIES

Agents:

SAINTS FAITH, HOPE, AND CHARITY

LIVED:
Second Century

FEAST DAY:
September 17

MISSION:
Tell people about Jesus.
Fight for the Faith.
Become martyrs for Christ.

It is hard to know what someone will do in an emergency. Some who seem strong might run away. Others who seem shy or weak might rise to the challenge and end up helping out the most.

35

Agents Faith, Hope, and Charity were three sisters who were all fierce agents of Christ. They told others about Jesus, with their mother St. Sophia, even though it was against the law. When they were captured, they were offered their freedom if they would only worship a false god. They refused! They stood together as a family, fighting against the enemy. They learned the enemy wasn't the evil emperor, but Satan himself. These agents were young, but they fought to the death for the Lord.

Sometimes we have struggles in our families or with our friends, and enemies seem to attack us from all sides. The best way to face these challenges is by praying. Even our enemies need prayer. We're not fighting against the person, as our agents learned, but against the enemy of the world, the devil. It's easy to pray for the people we love, but God tells us also to pray for the people who hate us! If Jesus can pray for the people who nailed Him to the cross, we can trust Him to teach us to pray for everyone He created, family, friend, or enemy.

O Holy Saints Faith, Hope, and Charity, pray for all Christians everywhere that we will have right faith, that we will have hope in the resurrection and the world to come, and that we will be kind to everyone with our words and actions. Amen.

PRAYERS FOR FAMILY

Dear Lord, help me to be helpful in my family. Amen.

Lord God, teach me to be patient with everyone in my home. Amen.

Holy Father, please bless those in my home. Amen.

PRAYER OF A CHILD

Our Father in heaven, bless all those who take care of me. Help me to honor and obey them the way You want me to.

Give me the strength to do a good job no matter how big or small the work. Bring me friends that will help me follow You. Help me to walk away from anyone or anything that would keep me from following You. Show me how to live a life that pleases You so my life will bring You glory. Amen.

PRAYER FOR FRIENDSHIPS

Lord my God, help me to be a good friend. Amen.

Dear Jesus, help me to be a good example to my friends and show them Your love through my words and actions. Amen.

Thank You for friends. Amen.

PRAYER FOR ENEMIES

Lord Jesus Christ, please help me to show kindness to my enemies. Amen.

Dear Lord, help me to be quick to forgive those who are unkind to me. Amen.

Father, You love those who hate You. Help me to love them too. Amen.

PRAYER BEFORE GOING TO SCHOOL

O Lord my God, help me to pay attention in class today and learn what I need to learn. Amen.

Dear Lord Jesus, thank You for my teacher and help me to be helpful to those who teach me. Amen.

My Father in heaven, help me to follow You whether at church, home, or school. Amen.

OPERATION 5

PRAYERS FOR THE DEAD

AGENT:
SAINT LAZARUS

CODE NAME:
Friend of Christ

REMEMBERED:
Lazarus Saturday during Great Lent

LIVED:
New Testament

MISSION:
Brother of Mary and Martha. Friend to Jesus. Raised from the dead by Jesus after four days.

Lazarus was the brother of Mary and Martha, whom Jesus visited in the Gospel of Luke 10:38–41. After Jesus had left them, Lazarus got very sick. The sisters sent someone to go and get Jesus because they knew He could heal their brother. But Jesus didn't come right away, and by the time He got there, Lazarus had been dead for four days.

Mary and Martha were sad and crying. Their friends and neighbors were crying. Even Jesus was crying. Jesus went to the tomb of Lazarus and said, "Take away the stone." Mary and Martha were surprised because they knew the body would already smell very bad. But they listened to Jesus and had the stone removed. Jesus said, "Lazarus, come out!" and to their surprise—he did!

When someone dies, it can be a very sad thing. Jesus cried for His friend even though He knew He would raise him from the dead. It is okay for us to cry when someone we love dies. There is a song we sing at the tomb right before Pascha that says, "The dead shall arise. Those in the tombs shall awake, all those on earth shall greatly rejoice." We pray for the dead because we have hope in the Resurrection of Christ.

PRAYERS FOR THE DEAD

Father God, I am sad because _____ *has died. Please let him/her find rest in You. Amen. Lord, bless the soul of Your servant* _____. *Amen.*

Most Holy Lord, You are holy and good. Help me to serve You in this life so I can be with You forever in heaven. Amen.

Thank You, Jesus, that You died and rose again, "trampling down death by death and to those in the tomb giving life." Amen.

MY DEPARTED LOVED ONES

_____

_____

_____

_____

_____

_____

_____

_____

_____

_____

_____

_____

_____

_____

_____

May their memory be eternal!

SECURITY CHECK:
PREPARATION FOR CONFESSION

AGENT:

SAINT MOSES THE BLACK

CODE NAME:
Saint Moses the Ethiopian

LIVED:
Fourth Century

FEAST DAY:
August 28

MISSION:
Started as an enemy of Christ.
Former slave, former robber.
Converted monk, priest.
Forgiven much.

Agent Moses the Black spent part of his life as a slave. He escaped slavery and became a much-feared robber and murderer. Leading a gang of seventy-five other robbers, he was going to steal from a monastery. But when he got there, he met the abbot, who was kind to him. He left his old ways behind and became a monk.

43

At first he was tempted to go back to his old ways and couldn't stop thinking of all the wrong things he had done. One day he was confessing his sins, and he saw an angel holding a tablet on which all his sins were written. Each time he confessed a sin, the angel wiped it off the tablet. By the time he finished, the tablet was completely clean.

Confession is how we leave our old ways behind and make ourselves ready to be used as agents. Confessing to our priest is like getting clearance from the agent God has put in our lives to watch over us. Use the following Ten Commandments to help you do a security check to get rid of any "road blocks" that could get in the way of your mission. Part of your training is learning the "Agent Objectives." Objectives are goals that will help you break through road blocks in the future.

SECURITY CHECK 1

You shall have no other gods before Me
Love God more than anything or anyone else.

Road Blocks:
- Complaining against God
- Doubting the Christian faith or teachings of the Church
- Believing in untrue or magical things
- Not doing what God wants because someone might make fun of you

Agent Objective 1:
Believe in God the Father, Son, and Holy Spirit.

SECURITY CHECK 2

You shall not make for yourself any false idols
Don't make anything in your life more important than God.

Road Blocks:
- Making any person or thing more important than God

- Taking focus away from Jesus during church by talking to friends

Agent Objective 2:
Go to confession and take communion. Do what Jesus did.

SECURITY CHECK 3
You shall not take the name of the Lord your God in vain
Always use the name of the Lord with love and respect.

Road Blocks:
- Using God's Holy Name in a wrong way
- Speaking badly about anyone

Agent Objective 3:
Be respectful of holy things and holy people.

SECURITY CHECK 4
Remember the Sabbath day and keep it holy
Follow God's example and rest on Sunday.

Road Blocks:
- Staying away from church on Sunday when you could have gone
- Doing work that doesn't need to be done on Sunday
- Spending Sunday doing sinful things

Agent Objective 4:
Keep the fasts and feasts the Church tells us to keep.

SECURITY CHECK 5
Honor your father and mother
Show love and respect to those who take care of you.

Road Blocks:
- Being sneaky or lying to parents or those care for you
- Choosing not to be helpful to those who care for you

Agent Objective 5:
Obey with a smile. Be kind and loving to brothers and sisters. Honor God by treating others with kindness.

SECURITY CHECK 6
You shall not murder
Never hurt anyone with actions, angry words, or angry thoughts.

Road Blocks:

- Using angry actions
- Using angry words
- Having angry thoughts
- Ignoring someone who needs help
- Hurting an animal

Agent Objective 6:
Kind words, gentle hands, good thoughts.

SECURITY CHECK 7
Do not commit adultery
You're not married yet, but when you are, be faithful to your husband or wife.

Road Blocks:
- Helping others to do sinful things
- Doing any sinful action alone or with others

Agent Objective 7:
Keep eyes, ears, and mouth from seeing, listening to, or doing any sinful thing.

SECURITY CHECK 8
Do not steal
Don't take anything that doesn't belong to you.

Road Blocks:
- Taking something that's not yours
- Keeping anything that's not yours
- Cheating anyone
- Wasting time, money, or things that belong to you

Agent Objective 8:
Pay everyone what you owe them. Give to those in need. Try to find the owners of things you find.

SECURITY CHECK 9
You shall not bear false witness against your neighbor
Don't lie about anyone.

Road Blocks:
- Telling lies or changing the truth to sound more exciting
- Telling secrets shared with you
- Telling bad stories about another person
- Covering up the truth

Agent Objective 9:
Let your words be kind. Never keep a "secret" that is an emergency or could hurt someone.

SECURITY CHECK 10
You shall not covet
Be happy with what you have, and be happy for other people when they get things.

Road Blocks:

- Being unhappy when something good happens to someone else
- Wishing for anything that belongs to someone else
- Destroying something that belongs to someone else
- Wishing for things God has not given you
- Being upset that God has not given you "more"
- Wanting someone to lose so you can get what they have

Agent Objective 10:

Share when you can. Be thankful for what God has given you. Be happy when good things happen to others.

ARMED AND READY:
WATCH OUT FOR THE ENEMY'S TRICKS

Agents have to be careful out there. The enemy doesn't care how old you are; he only knows you are working for Jesus and wants you destroyed. One way he tricks agents of Christ is by making sin not look like sin. You may know when you sin, but the enemy doesn't want us to think about how we help others to sin.

You are helping someone to sin when:

- You encourage someone to sin: "Go ahead, do it"
- You force someone to do something sinful: "Do that or I'll beat you up"
- You tell someone it's okay to do something sinful: "Yes, it's okay if you do that"
- You challenge or dare someone to sin: "I double dare you to do that"
- You show you like it when someone sins: "Oh, that was awesome!"
- You help to hide someone's sin: "Hide over here so they don't find out"
- You sin together with another person: "Yes, let's both do it!"

- You keep a dangerous secret: "Don't worry, I won't tell"*

Sometimes a Special Agent has to do hard things. It is not being a good friend to keep a dangerous secret. Tell a grown-up you trust right away!

Now that you've looked at all the security checks (commandments), pushed through the road blocks, and understood your objective (goal), it's time to pray and ask God to show you if you've left anything out. Sometimes there are private or scary things you might be afraid to tell the priest, but God is not surprised by anything, and there is nothing you could ever do to stop Him from loving you. He tells us that when we confess, He gets rid of our sin and, like St. Moses', our hearts get wiped clean.

A PRAYER OF REPENTANCE
(sorrow for what I have done wrong)

You, O Lord, are full of forgiveness. I am sorry for all the sinful things I've thought, said, or done. My sin makes my heart sad, and I pray to You, O Lord, to forgive me of all my past sins and save me from them. I know I can only change with Your help, so I am asking You to show me how to change what I have been doing and walk away from my sin so I can walk in Your ways. In the Name of the Father, Son, and Holy Spirit. Amen.

PRAYER AFTER CONFESSION

O powerful and forgiving God, I am so thankful You have taken away my sins. Bless me, O Lord, and help me always, so I will do what You want me to do and walk away from sin. Amen.

PRAYING WITH THE SAINTS AND ANGELS

What if you needed help with something you just couldn't do by yourself? What would you do? You'd probably ask someone to help you. We can always ask God to help us with anything, but He has also given us the saints to ask for help. It is like calling another agent and asking them to come over and give you a hand. Their example and their prayers can make us feel better and help us through the hardest missions.

HYMN TO THE THEOTOKOS

This song we sing in church reminds us that it is a good thing to remember that the Theotokos is holy, even more than the angels, because she is the Holy Mother of Jesus. Remember these words and see if you can hear them at church.

It is truly right to bless you, O Theotokos, ever blessed and all-blameless and the mother of our God. More honorable than the cherubim and more glorious beyond compare than the seraphim, without corruption you gave birth to God the Word. True Theotokos, we magnify you.

51

PRAYER TO YOUR GUARDIAN ANGEL

O angel of God, my holy guardian, given to me from heaven, guard me this day and save me from all evil. Instruct me in doing good deeds, and set me on the path of salvation. Amen.

O angel of Christ, holy guardian and protector of my soul and body, forgive me for any way I may have offended you every day of my life, and protect me from all forms of pressure and temptation of the evil one. May I never again anger God by my sins. Pray for me to the Lord, that He may make me worthy of the grace of the All-holy Trinity, and of the blessed Mother of God, and of all the saints. Amen.

A PRAYER TO YOUR SAINT

Pray to God for me, O Holy Saint _____, for you bring God joy: I turn to you, who are a fast helper and one who prays to God for the salvation of my soul.

INTO THE FIRE
The Three Holy Youths

AGENTS:

HANANIAH, AZARIAH, MISHAEL

CODE NAMES:
Shadrach, Meshach, Abednego

FEAST DAY:
December 17

LIVED:
Old Testament (Daniel 1–3)

MISSION:
Stolen along with Agent Daniel. Wise youths. Refuse to bow before a false god. Survive fiery furnace!

O Holy Youths, you who stood for our Lord even when faced with death, I am afraid and I need help to trust the Lord to save me. Pray to the Lord for me.

YOU FIGHT LIKE A GIRL
St. Katherine of Alexandria (Egypt)

AGENT:

ST. KATHERINE

LIVED:
Fourth Century

FEAST DAY:
November 24

MISSION:
Argue and win against 50 wise men, 200 guards, and the empress. Thrown in jail. Survived tortures. At age 18, fought for the faith to the death.

Holy Great Martyr Katherine, pray to God for us!

Troparion (Tone 5)
Let us praise Katherine, the glowing bride of Jesus, protector of Sinai and our helper. By the power of the Holy Spirit, she shut the prideful mouths of those who did not believe in God. She wears the crown of a saint who fought to the death, and asks God to forgive us all.

DRAGON SLAYER
St. George

AGENT:

ST. GEORGE

CODE NAME:
George the Victory-Bearer

FEAST DAY:
April 23

LIVED:
Third Century

MISSION:
Secret Christian.
Commander in the Roman army.
Soldier for Christ.
Killed a dragon. Defender of
the faith to the death.

Kontakion (Tone 4)
God raised you as his own gardener, O George, for you have collected for yourself virtues. Having planted in tears, you now harvest with joy; you shed your blood in battle and won Christ as your crown. Through your prayers, forgiveness of sins is granted to all.

LEADERS OF THE HEAVENLY ARMIES
Archangels Gabriel and Michael

COVERT AGENT:
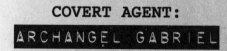
ARCHANGEL GABRIEL

LIVES:
Unknown beginning

FEAST DAYS:
March 26 & July 13

MISSION:
Leader of the heavenly hosts.
Appeared to Agent Daniel.
Messenger to Zechariah,
the father of John the Baptist.
Messenger to the Theotokos.

Supreme Leader of the heavenly host, I beg you that by your prayers you will surround us with the protection of your heavenly glory, and guard us who cry out to you for your protection. Deliver us from all dangers, for you are the commander of the powers above.

COVERT AGENT:
ARCHANGEL MICHAEL

LIVES:
Unknown beginning

FEAST DAY:
November 8

MISSION:
Chief commander of the
heavenly hosts.
Messenger to Agent Joshua.
Fought alongside Archangel
Gabriel.

Troparion (Tone 1)
Let us praise cherubim, seraphim, thrones, powers, authorities and principalities, dominions, archangels, and angels, for they are the bodiless ministers of the Holy Trinity and revealers of mysteries we don't understand. Glory to Him who has given you being; glory to Him who

has given you light; glory to Him who is praised by you in thrice-holy hymns.

CARETAKER OF THE POOR
St. Brigid of Kildare

AGENT:

ST. BRIGID OF KILDARE

LIVED:
Fifth Century

Feast Day:
February 1

MISSION:
Care for the poor.
Lighten everyone's burden.
Comfort the suffering.

O Holy Saint Brigid, you whose wish it was to care for the suffering, pray to the Lord for me in my time of trouble.

PROTECTOR OF CHILDREN
St. Nicholas the Wonderworker

AGENT:

**ST. NICHOLAS
THE WONDERWORKER**

LIVED:
Fourth Century

FEAST DAY:
December 6

MISSION:
Kept three sisters out of slavery with gold secretly given. Protector of children. Wonderworker.

O Nicholas, bless us; bless your people who, before God and before you, humbly stand in prayer. Amen.

Troparion (Tone 4)
Your works of justice showed you to your congregation a canon of faith, the likeness of humility, a teacher of abstinence, O Father, Bishop Nicholas. Wherefore, by humility you achieved exaltation, and by meekness, richness. Intercede, therefore, with Christ to save our souls.

MODERN–DAY SAINTS

Martyr of San Francisco

AGENT:

LIVED:
Nineteenth Century

FEAST DAY:
September 24

MISSION:
14-year-old who kept the Orthodox faith to the death!

Holy Saint Peter, pray to God for us.

Wonderworker of Shanghai and San Francisco

AGENT:
ST. JOHN MAXIMOVICH

LIVED:
Twentieth Century

FEAST DAY:
July 2

MISSION:
**Cared for orphans.
Miracle worker.
Prayer warrior.**

You pray for the whole world, O Holy St. John, holy wonderworker for God. Come quickly to my aid as I honor you with my whole heart. Be a speedy helper in my time of need, you who are a lover of God.

Good Shepherd of the Lost Sheep in America

AGENT:
ST. RAPHAEL OF BROOKLYN

LIVED:
Twentieth Century

FEAST DAYS:
**First Saturday in
November & February 27**

MISSION:
**Tireless traveler for Christ.
Planter of churches.
Friend to the poor.**

Troparion

Rejoice, O Father Raphael, adornment of the holy Church. You are the champion of the true faith, seeker of the lost, relief of the helpless, father to orphans, friend of the poor, peacemaker and good shepherd, joy of all the Orthodox, son of Antioch, treasure of America: intercede with Christ God for us and for all who honor you.

First Native American Priest

AGENT:

ST. JACOB NETSVETOV

LIVED:
Nineteenth Century

FEAST DAY:
July 26

MISSION:
Missionary for Christ.
Healer of sickness and
terror of demons.

Troparion

O righteous father Jacob, healer of sickness and terror of demons, pray to Christ God that our souls may be saved.

OPERATION 8

PRAY LIKE A KING

AGENT:

ST. DAVID

LIVED:
Old Testament

FEAST DAY:
Sunday after Nativity

WROTE:
Most of the Book of Psalms

MISSION:
Care for sheep. Kill a lion.
Defeat a giant. Become king,
musician, writer, and
man after God's own heart.

God is amazing! He has chosen agents to serve Him that others wouldn't even consider, like Agent David. When David was a boy, his family was visited by another agent, Samuel, Prophet of God. Samuel had been sent to find a new king. David's brothers were big and strong, but they were not the one God had chosen. Samuel was surprised when he saw the young boy David and was sure God couldn't mean him. But He did.

Even though God called him "a man after my own heart," when Agent David became king he faced many challenges. Some of his challenges were from enemies and some from his own sins. David wrote the Psalms as prayers and songs to thank God for His goodness and to call out to the Lord for help. We can use the Psalms to help us pray and as a reminder that God is our help always!

» *To find out more about David, the agent who was a king, read 1 and 2 Samuel in your Bible.*

Psalm 3:1–4
Lord, I have so many enemies!
So many people are rising up against me!
Many are saying about me,
"God will not save him."
Lord, you are like a shield that keeps me safe.
You honor me. You help me win the battle.
I call out to the Lord.
He answers me from his holy hill.

Psalm 4:1
My faithful God,
answer me when I call out to you.
Give me rest from my trouble.
Show me your favor. Hear my prayer.

Psalm 4:4
When you are angry, do not sin.
When you are in bed,
look deep down inside you and be silent.
Selah (means: stop and think about this)

Psalm 5:3
Lord, in the morning you hear my voice.
In the morning I pray to you.
I wait for you in hope.

Psalm 7:10
The Most High God is like a shield that keeps me safe.
He saves those whose hearts are honest.

Psalm 13:5–6
But I trust in your faithful love.
My heart is filled with joy because you will save me.
I will sing to the Lord.
He has been so good to me.

Psalm 18:1–3
I love you, Lord.
You give me strength.
The Lord is my rock and my fort. He is the One who
    saves me.
My God is my rock. I go to him for safety.
He is like a shield to me. He's the power that saves me.
    He's my place of safety.
I call out to the Lord. He is worthy of praise.
He saves me from my enemies.

Psalm 19:14
Lord, may the words of my mouth and the thoughts of
    my heart
be pleasing in your eyes.
You are my Rock and my Redeemer.

Psalm 24:7–10 NKJV
This psalm is used at Pascha.
Lift up your heads, O you gates!
And be lifted up, you everlasting doors!
And the King of glory shall come in.
Who is this King of glory?
The Lord strong and mighty,
The Lord mighty in battle.
Lift up your heads, O you gates!
Lift up, you everlasting doors!
And the King of glory shall come in.

Who is this King of glory?
The LORD of hosts,
He is the King of glory.

Psalm 25:16
Turn to me and show me your favor.
I am lonely and hurting.

Psalm 25:20
Guard my life. Save me.
Don't let me be put to shame.
I go to you for safety.

Psalm 28:9 *NKJV*
Save Your people,
And bless Your inheritance;
Shepherd them also,
And bear them up forever.

Psalm 29:11
The Lord gives strength to his people.
The Lord blesses his people with peace.

Psalm 31:9
Lord, show me your favor. I'm in deep trouble.
I'm so sad I can hardly see.
My whole body grows weak with sadness.

Psalm 34:4
I looked to the Lord, and he answered me.
He saved me from everything I was afraid of.

Psalm 34:8
Taste and see that the Lord is good.
Blessed is the man who goes to him for safety.

Psalm 35:18
I will give you thanks in the whole community.
Among all of your people I will praise you.

Psalm 46:1
God is our place of safety. He gives us strength.
He is always there to help us in times of trouble.

Psalm 47:7
God is the King of the whole earth.
Sing a psalm of praise to him.

Psalm 91:1–2
God, show me your favor
in keeping with your faithful love.
Because your love is so tender and kind,
wipe out my lawless acts.
Wash away all of the evil things I've done.
Make me pure from my sin.

Psalm 62:1–2
I find my rest in God alone.
He is the One who saves me.
He alone is my rock. He is the One who saves me.
He is like a fort to me. I will always be secure.

Psalm 84:1–4
Lord who rules over all,
how lovely is the place where you live!
I long to be in the courtyards of the Lord's temple.
I deeply long to be there.
My whole being cries out
for the living God.
Lord who rules over all,
even the sparrow has found a home near your altar.
My King and my God,
the swallow also has a nest there,
where she may have her young.

Blessed are those who live in your house.
They are always praising you.

Psalm 91:1–2

The person who rests in the shadow of the Most High God
will be kept safe by the Mighty One.
I will say about the Lord,
"He is my place of safety.
He is like a fort to me.
He is my God. I trust in him."

Psalm 95:2–6

Let us come to him and give him thanks.
Let us praise him with music and song.
The Lord is the great God.
He is the greatest King.
He rules over all of the gods.
He owns the deepest parts of the earth.
The mountain peaks belong to him.
The ocean is his, because he made it.
He formed the dry land with his hands.
Come, let us bow down and worship him.
Let us fall on our knees in front of the Lord our Maker.

Psalm 102:1–2

Lord, hear my prayer.
Listen to my cry for help.
Don't turn your face away from me
when I'm in trouble.
Pay attention to me.
When I call out for help, answer me quickly.

Psalm 106:4

Lord, remember me when you show favor to your people.
Help me when you save them.

Psalm 108:5
God, may you be honored above the heavens.
Let your glory be over the whole earth.

Psalm 117
All you nations, praise the Lord.
All you people on earth, praise him.
Great is his love for us.
The Lord is faithful forever.
Praise the Lord.

Psalm 134
All of you who serve the Lord, praise the Lord.
All of you who serve at night in the house of the Lord,
    praise him.

Psalm 140:4
Lord, keep me out of the hands of sinful people.
Keep me safe from men who want to hurt me.
They plan to trip me up and make me fall.

Psalm 148:1
Praise the Lord.
Praise the Lord from the heavens.
Praise him in the heavens above.

PART TWO

TRAINING

THE FIVE TRAINING TARGETS

THE FIVE SENSES

An agent of Christ is always in training. We are always using all of our senses to learn whatever God might have for us to learn so we can be ready for every mission. Each time we go to the Divine Liturgy, we are secretly being trained so we can go out and face the challenges of each week. God uses five targets to get our attention. See if you can spot any of these targets used in weekly training. If you can, you're on your way to being an amazing agent of Christ!

TASTE

"Taste and see that the Lord is good." (Psalm 34:8)

We use our mouths when we take the Body and Blood of Christ. That Body and Blood is for an agent's healing, inside and out.

71

SMELL

"May my prayer come to you like the sweet smell of incense. When I lift up my hands in prayer, may it be like the evening sacrifice." (Psalm 141:2)

The church has a smell that is different from anywhere else. I bet even if you were blindfolded, you would know the moment you entered a church, just because of your wonderful nose! When I go to a fast food place, I smell hamburgers and French fries. Those smells prepare my mind to eat. When I go to a field to play soccer, I smell grass. That smell prepares my mind to run hard and focus on trying to make a goal. But when I smell incense at church, it tells my mind I am somewhere holy, and it prepares my mind for God.

TOUCH

"She said to herself, 'if only I touch His cloak, I will be healed.'" (Matthew 9:21)

We use our hands and our bodies in our training. We kiss the icons in the church. Sometimes we bow low to the ground in worship. We cross ourselves, showing the world whom we serve. We reach out and touch the robes of the priest, just as the woman in the Bible reached out in faith, touched the robes of Christ, and was made well.

HEAR

"Let Christ's word live in you like a rich treasure. Teach and correct each other wisely. Sing psalms, hymns, and spiritual songs. Sing with thanks in your hearts to God." (Colossians 3:16)

In our training, we use our ears for a lot of things. When we enter a church for a service, we usually hear singing, chanting, or talking. The choir is important in our training because they are leading us in worship. It is also their job to help us respond to the prayers the deacon or priest is praying during the liturgy. That's why we sing, "Lord, have mercy," so many times.

The chanters help us learn about the saint of the day and the feasts we are celebrating. Chanting is different from singing, just as icons look different from a regular picture. Chanting helps us hear the truth of God just as icons help us see and understand things about a saint.

We hear the words of the priest during the homily as he teaches us how to live like agents. We hear the bells on the censer and the big bells some churches have because every Sunday is a celebration of the Resurrection of Christ.

SEE

"Lord, now let Your servant depart in peace, according to Your word; for my eyes have seen Your salvation, which You have prepared before the face of all people; a light to enlighten the Gentiles, and the glory of Your people Israel." (Luke 2:29–32, liturgical translation)

We use our eyes to see the icons, which remind us of all the agents we are serving with. We see the beauty of the temple we worship in, which reminds us of heaven. We see the incense rising, which reminds us of the prayers going up to the throne of God. Through the Liturgy we are able to see the salvation of the Lord.

Taste, Hear, Smell, Touch, and See if you can discover the amazing undercover training you can get during the Divine Liturgy.

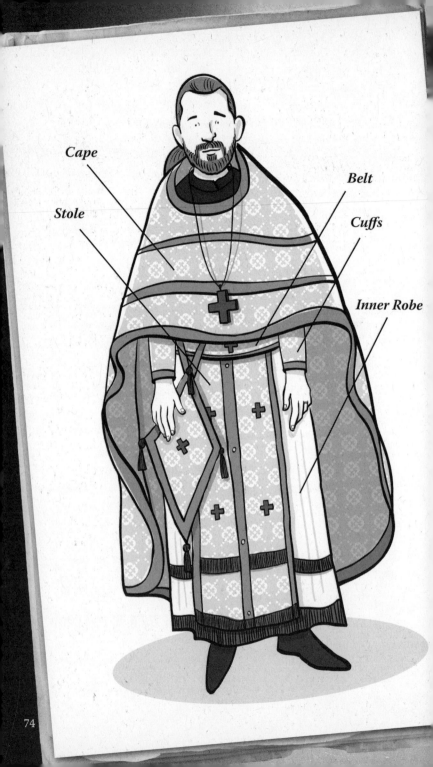

Cape

Stole

Belt

Cuffs

Inner Robe

AGENT ATTIRE
PRIESTS AND WHY THEY WEAR WHAT THEY WEAR

AN UNBROKEN CHAIN: FROM APOSTLES TO PRIESTS

Jesus picked His apostles to be special agents for Him. After he rose from the dead, He gave them a command to go into all the world and tell everyone about Himself. He told them to baptize in the name of the Father and the Son and the Holy Spirit (Matthew 28:19–20). These agents of Christ did just what Jesus told them to do—they told everyone about the Cross and that Jesus was no longer dead but ALIVE!

There were so many people who believed and were baptized that there couldn't be an apostle for every church. They needed help. God brought the apostles godly men to serve in their place. They prayed and laid their hands on those men, and made them priests.

After the apostles, those agents who had taken up the mission of the apostles needed help. These bishops laid hands on godly men and made them priests to serve Christ's holy Church. This happened over and over again from the hands of the Apostles all the way to your

75

patriarch, your metropolitan, your bishop, and your priest. That's a giant chain of agents reaching from your church all the way back to God's Special Forces—the Apostles!

A priest of Christ is a very special agent. He is the one God has sent to train young agents in battle. When we go into church, we hear things, see things, smell things, taste things, and touch things. One of the things we see is the priest. The clothing he wears to serve the Liturgy isn't just what he happens to have in the closet. The things he wears have meaning, and the colors tell us what we're celebrating in the Church.

Before a priest even starts to dress he says this prayer, taken from part of Psalm 5:7:

"I will enter Your House and in Your fear, I will worship toward Your Holy Temple."

INNER ROBE

This long robe shows the purity of heart the priest is supposed to have. When the priest puts on this robe, he says the following prayer:

"My soul shall exult in the Lord, for He has endued [dressed] me with the robe of salvation, and with the garment of joy has He clothed me. He has set a crown on my head like a bridegroom, and like a bride He has adorned me with comeliness [beauty]." (Isaiah 61:10)

STOLE

The stole reminds us of the grace God gives a priest. It also reminds us of the Cross Jesus carried on His shoulders. It is the only vestment that must always be worn. When putting on the stole, the priest says:

"Blessed is God, who pours His grace on His priests, like the balm [oil] on the head, that ran down the beard, even Aaron's beard, down to the skirts of his garment." (Psalm 133:2)

BELT

The belt is worn over the inner robe and the stole. The belt shows that the priest is ready to serve and to get the strength he needs from the Holy Spirit to succeed in his mission. When the priest puts on the belt, he says:

"Blessed is God, who girds [binds] me with strength, and makes my way perfect." (Psalm 18:32)

CUFFS

The cuffs help take the focus off the hands of the priest himself and tell us that those hands have been set aside to touch the body of the Lord in the Eucharist. Since the cuffs are only worn for the Eucharist (when a priest has all his vestments on), they show us the priest is serving as the hands of Christ to His people. When putting on the first cuff, the priest prays:

"Your right hand, O Lord, is glorified in strength. Your right hand, O Lord, has shattered the enemy, and through the multitude of Your glory You have crushed Your adversaries [enemies]." (Exodus 15:6–7)

When putting on the second cuff he says:

"Your hands have made me and molded [formed] me; give me understanding, and I will learn Your Commandments." (Psalm 119:73)

CAPE

The cape reminds us of the robe the soldiers put on Jesus to make fun of Him as "king of the Jews" just before He was nailed to the cross. The priest places the cape over his head and says:

"Let Your priests be clothed with righteousness; and let Your saints shout for joy, always, now and ever, and to the ages of ages. Amen." (Psalm 132:9)

After putting on all his vestments, the priest washes his hands to show he is clean, and says:

"I will wash my hands among the innocent, and so will I go round Your altar, O Lord." (Psalm 26:6)

Now the priest, as a special agent of Christ, is ready to serve the Divine Liturgy.

COLOR CODE
What the different vestment colors mean

There are secret codes that every agent in training should know. These color codes let you know what is going on during the church year without anyone having to tell you anything! Study these codes to become a master in this area of training.

- **Gold** means we are celebrating Jesus, the Prophets, Apostles, or Holy Hierarchs
- **Red** means we are remembering the Cross of Our Lord, those who have died for the sake of Christ (martyrs), or Nativity
- **Blue** robes tell us we are celebrating the Theotokos (Panagia)
- **Black/Purple** robes are worn during Great Lent and Holy Week. Lent is a time of bright sadness as we walk with Christ through His life to His death on the cross. Thankfully we know Pascha is coming!
- **Green** is worn at Pentecost, 50 days after Pascha
- **White** is worn for funerals and Pascha

SPECIAL AGENTS OF CHRIST

1 TIMOTHY 4:12

DRILL TWO: AGENT ATTIRE——PRIESTS AND WHY THEY WEAR WHAT THEY WEAR

SORE FEET FOR THE KINGDOM

THE LITURGY

MEDIC ALERT

Why we go to church

Did you know the Church is like a hospital? We don't go there to fix broken bones, but we do go there to fix broken thinking and feelings. Sometimes life is really hard. Sometimes our thoughts or feelings catch a cold sent by the enemy. We go to church so we can get the "medicine" we need through confession and the Eucharist (communion). Before we take the Eucharist, we say we believe that the wine and bread are really the body and blood of Jesus and we take that "medicine" for the forgiveness of our sins and for never-ending life. We also go to church when we feel good, because it helps keep us strong on the inside so we can fight against the enemy.

A TOUCHING STORY
Why we touch the priest's robes

Have you ever wondered why we touch the priest's robes when he walks around the church? Here's the story:

Just then a woman came up behind Jesus. She had a sickness that made her bleed. It had lasted for twelve years. She touched the edge of his clothes. She thought, "I only need to touch his clothes. Then I will be healed." (Matthew 9:20–21)

Can you imagine bleeding for 12 years? Over the years this woman had been to lots of doctors and spent all her money but never got well. It took great faith for her to reach out and touch Jesus' robes. When we reach out and touch the robes of the priest, we are reaching out in faith too, believing that Jesus hears our prayers and can make us well.

A SIGN FOR THE TIMES
Why we cross ourselves

Did you know crossing yourself is telling the world who God is and whom we belong to? When we cross ourselves, we hold our hands in a way that says something. We put our thumb, pointer, and middle fingers together to say that we believe in the Father, the Son, and the Holy Spirit. The ring finger and pinky stay down on our palm to say we believe Jesus was fully God and fully man. When we touch our head, we're saying we love God with all our mind. When we touch our chest, we're saying we love God with all our heart. When we touch our right shoulder, then our left, we're saying we love God with all our strength or power. When we cross ourselves, the enemy of the world runs away in fear, because he knows that Jesus wins.

THROUGH THE THEOTOKOS
Blessed Mary

Many of our agents had amazing things happen to them. Agent Daniel survived the lions' den, the Three Holy Children survived fire, King David killed a giant. But there was one agent who did something no other agent has done or ever will do again. This agent gave birth to God!

Now, God was always there, so she didn't make or create God, but she carried inside her body the One who created the entire universe when He came to earth as a baby. When the angel came to Mary and told her she was going to have a baby and that baby was going to be Jesus, God's Son, did she have a choice? Yes, she did have a choice. She could have said no. God gives everyone a choice to follow Him or not. We are thankful Mary said YES!

We bless Mary because she is the mother of our King and our God. We call her the Theotokos because it means "God-Bearer." She is also called Panagia (pan-uh-**gee**-uh) because it means "all holy" or "all holy of all the saints." The Church teaches that Mary is the best person who ever lived. This is why she was chosen to be the Mother of God's Son. Only Jesus is more holy than Mary.

TAKE A STAND
Why we stand during the entire Eucharist

If you are reading this book, you are old enough to challenge yourself to stand during the entire church service. When you stand, you are using your body to pray. It seems like a long time, and legs do get tired, but this is part of your training. As you are building those leg muscles by standing a little longer each week, there are some important times to make sure you always stand.

- At the beginning of the service when we hear "Blessed is the Kingdom . . ."

- When the deacon and priest come out with the Bible
- During the Gospel reading
- During the Great Entrance when the priest walks around the church with the bread and wine
- During the Creed and the Lord's Prayer
- During the entire Eucharist

But why stand for the entire Eucharist? After the priest walks around the church with the bread and wine, he takes them back behind the altar. He says some prayers and holds up the wine and bread. He is asking the Holy Spirit to make the bread and wine into the body and blood of Jesus.

Matthew 26:26–28 says:

"And as they were eating, Jesus took bread, blessed and broke it, and gave it to the disciples and said, "Take, eat; this is My body." Then He took the cup, and gave thanks, and gave it to them, saying, "Drink from it, all of you. For this is My blood of the new covenant [promise], which is shed for many for the remission [forgiveness] of sins." (NKJV)

When the priest comes out with the cup to give us the Eucharist, he is no longer holding wine and bread but the very body and blood of Jesus. And since we are in the presence of our King and our God, we show respect by standing until the priest takes the cup back to the altar.

DON'T LET ANYONE LOOK DOWN ON YOU BECAUSE YOU'RE YOUNG

LIVE LIKE AN AGENT

AGENT:

PROPHET SAMUEL

LIVED:
Old Testament

FEAST DAY:
August 20

MISSION:
Served the Lord as a very young child. Heard the voice of the Lord calling his name. Made a shepherd named David King of Israel.

Samuel went to live at the temple and be trained by priests when he was very little. As he grew, he began to hear God's voice. At first he thought it was the high priest Eli calling his name, but it turned out to be God! Later, God used him to find a boy named David and make him king. Samuel started out as a young child in the service of God, and through simple prayer and obedience, grew to be a great prophet.

Sometimes it can be so hard to be young. You see all the things teenagers and adults can do to serve the Lord. But what can you do?

God doesn't make us wait until we're older to serve Him. Throughout the Bible and the lives of the saints, we see many examples of children who showed amazing courage and strength when they had to do hard things. St. Paul tells St. Timothy:

"Don't let anyone look down on you because you are young. Set an example for the believers in what you say and in how you live. Also set an example in how you love and in what you believe. Show the believers how to be pure." 1 Timothy 4:12

You are old enough right now to set an example in what you say and how you live. You are old enough right now to set an example in how you love and in what you believe. You are old enough right now to be an agent of Christ.

There might be some words in this book or some words you say in church you might not know the meaning of. There are lots of grown-ups who might not know the meaning either. It's helpful as an agent to know what you are saying so you know what you are telling the world that you believe.

Acknowledge: To agree something is true

All-Comely: Good looking. Patriarch Joseph is called "All-Comely," but he wasn't only good-looking on the outside—he was beautiful on the inside, too. "Man looks on the outside but God looks at the heart" (1 Samuel 16:7b).

Apostolic: The way of the apostles or the way the apostles did things

Ascend: To go up

Cleanse: Make clean

Covert: Undercover

Creed: "I believe." The Nicene Creed is the statement of the Church's faith.

Crucify: To torture and kill by nailing to a cross

Dwell: To live in. We ask Jesus to dwell/live in us.

Essence: Basic nature or being

Eucharist: (**you**-kuh-rist) Holy Communion

Hallowed: Holy

Hymn: A song of joy and praise to God

Immortal: Everlasting, eternal, without death

Incarnate: Made into flesh and blood. Jesus was incarnate when He became man.

Infirmities: Weakness or sickness of body or soul/heart

Iniquities: Sin or wrongdoing

Mercy: Undeserved kindness

One Holy Catholic and Apostolic Church: The One Church as it was handed down to the apostles by Jesus and to us by the Apostles

Only-Begotten Son: The only Son who shares the nature of the Father and has existed forever. All other sons are created.

Panagia: (pan-uh-**gee**-uh) All-holy—talking about Mary the Mother of God

Proceeds: Goes out from

Psalm: Holy song

Remission: Forgiveness of sins

Repentance: Deep sadness for sin or wrong you have done

Testament: Testimony or witness of something true

Temptation: A trap the enemy sets to get you away from God

Theotokos: (thay-oh-**toh**-kose) "God-bearer": the name we use for Mary as the Mother of God

Treasury: Place where something valuable or costly is kept

Trespass: To sin, do wrong, or break the law

Trisagion: (try-**sah**-gee-on) Three times holy or thrice holy

Troparion: (tro-**par**-ee-on) Short hymn/song of joy or praise

Vestment: Special clothing worn by priests and deacons

ABOUT THE AUTHOR

Annalisa Boyd is mother to 6 and has fostered 25 children (so far). It is her desire for each child to be inspired to become an agent of Christ and embrace the faith of the Church as his or her own. Annalisa and her family reside in the beautiful foothills of the Rocky Mountains of Colorado. She is also the author of the popular teen prayer book from Conciliar Press, *Hear Me.*

ALSO BY THE AUTHOR

Hear Me: A Prayerbook for Orthodox Teens
Compiled and edited by Annalisa Boyd

Hear Me is a prayer book designed to address the unique challenges Orthodox youth experience in their walk with Christ. This user-friendly manual communicates the importance of both corporate and personal prayer. Prayers for school, friendships, and family give teens tools for successful relationships. A topical section offers encouragement as teens face daily challenges. The Q & A section answers practical questions. *Hear Me* gives teens direction in using the tools Christ has given us—Holy Scripture as the map, and the Church and her Traditions the compass, helping our youth find their own path toward theosis.

• Paperback, 96 pages (ISBN: 978-1-888212-93-8)
CP Order number 007446—$8.95*

* Price does not include applicable sales tax or shipping and handling.

To request a Conciliar Press catalog, to obtain complete ordering information, or to place a credit card order, please call Conciliar Press at (800) 967-7377 or log onto our website: www.conciliarpress.com.

Conciliar Media Ministries hopes you have enjoyed and benefited from this book. The proceeds from the sales of our books only partially cover the costs of operating our nonprofit ministry—which includes both the work of Conciliar Press and the work of Ancient Faith Radio. Your financial support makes it possible to continue this ministry both in print and online. Donations are tax-deductible and can be made at www.ancientfaith.com.

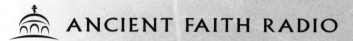

ANCIENT FAITH RADIO

Internet-Based Orthodox Radio:
Podcasts, 24-hour music and talk stations,
teaching, conference recordings, and much more,
at www.ancientfaith.com